South East Rhymes

Edited By Lawrence Smith

First published in Great Britain in 2018 by:

 Young**Writers**

Young Writers
Remus House
Coltsfoot Drive
Peterborough
PE2 9BF
Telephone: 01733 890066
Website: www.youngwriters.co.uk

FOREWORD

Young Writers was established in 1991, dedicated to encouraging reading and creative writing in young people. Our nationwide writing initiatives are designed to inspire ideas and give pupils the incentive to write, and in turn develop literacy skills and confidence, whilst participating in a fun, imaginative activity.

Few things are more encouraging for the aspiring writer than seeing their own work in print, so we are proud that our anthologies are able to give young authors this unique sense of confidence and pride in their abilities.

For our latest competition, Rhymecraft, primary school pupils were asked to enter a land of poetry where they used poetic techniques such as rhyme, simile and alliteration to bring their ideas to life. The result is an entertaining and imaginative anthology which will make a charming keepsake for years to come.

Each poem showcases the creativity and talent of these budding new writers as they learn the skills of writing, and we hope you are as entertained by them as we are.

CONTENTS

Aliyah Jones (10)	63	Archy Frogley (7)	103
Zahra Amir (0)	64	Nevaeh Collier (7)	104
Sahib Singh Sond	65	Sian Donnelly (7)	105
Kayan Zorba (9)	66	Tallulah Wevers (7)	106
Yashika Pandey (10)	67	Rosie-Jane Bateman (7)	107
Ava Dhadwal (7)	68	Emma Grace Laybourn (8)	108
Ayaan Ahmed (9)	69	Amy Horncastle (8)	109
Connie May Shell (7)	70	Lewis Daniel Hatchett (8)	110
Vikram Singh (10)	71	Ellsie Webb (7)	111
Archie Batts (10)	72	Christopher Mann (7)	112
Madison Roundacre (7)	73	Paige Louise Willis (7)	113
Luke Moore (10)	74	Billy Webb (7)	114
Donnell Lemar Lucky-Oligie	75	Frazer Wilson-Green (7)	115
Amber Starling (9)	76	Anthony Rawles (8)	116
Shasvathan Uthayakumaran (9)	77	Lucas Gibson (8)	117
Danyaal Ahmed (9)	78	Jake Hurst (7)	118
Jayden Gable Williams (10)	79	Ronnie Jay Garland (8)	119
Jack Grimsey (9)	80	Samuel Munro (7)	120
Ruth Anne Leonce (8)	81	Jamie Vice (8)	121
Maanav Aravindan	82	Ruby Fitzgerald (7)	122
Riti Limani (7)	83	Max Bridges (8)	123
		Teddy Vallis (8)	124

Graham James Primary School, Corringham

		Joshua Cannings (7)	125
		Tyler Griffiths (7)	126
		Henley Jackson (7)	127
Jessica O'Rourke (8)	84	Lukas James Shawyer (8)	128
Vinnie Turner (8)	85	Lexi Ridgewell (8)	129
Tommy Lewis Spears (8)	86	Charlie Finch (8)	130
Emily Kench (7)	87	Daisy Adela Anderson (8)	131
Adam Bassett (7)	88	Georgia Unwin (7)	132
Alfie Henry (7)	89	Marco Eric Minter (8)	133
Bobby Long (8)	90		
Tyler Thomas Oakley (7)	91		
Millie Farmer (7)	92	**Hedgewood School, Hayes**	
Regan Branch (7)	93		
Ellie-May Mannion (7)	94	Joshua Maxwell (10)	134
Callum Anderson (8)	95	Marcel Wyrzykowski (10)	135
Bobby Iceton (7)	96	Zak Bhad (11)	136
Lily Conquest (7)	97	Chris Byrne (10)	137
Aiden Kercher (7)	98	Emma Sofia Walsh (11)	138
Thomas Vallis (8)	99	Mohamed Jama (11)	139
Bethany Moore (8)	100	Rocky Verma (11)	140
James Baker (8)	101	Sam Fletcher (10)	141
Callie Strong (8)	102		

Ingatestone & Fryerning CE (VA) Junior School, Ingatestone

Ophelia Ruby Tucker (9)	142
Ruby Ann Kendell (9)	144
Tegan Barber (7)	146
Sophie Thomas-Scrine (11)	147
Ella Farrow (11) & Ava Farrow (9)	148
Orla (10) & Darcie Earp (10)	149
Jenson George Wiles (8)	150
Emily Sutton (10)	151
Poppy Edwards (10)	152
Imogen George (7)	153
Saffron Alexandra Burrows (7)	154
Ariana Knight (7)	155

Longfield Primary School, Harrow

Ziyan Khan (9)	156
Umika K Bhula (8)	157
Isa Khan (8)	158
Ayden Alam (8)	159
Shiven Patel (8)	160
Mili Jackson (10)	161

Manor Mead School, Shepperton

Eamon Aichaine (10)	162
Arun Dodson (11)	163

Rolph CE Primary School, Thorpe Le Soken

Olive Yardley (8)	164
Jessica Arnold (8)	165
Toby Hamer (7)	166
Amelia Jane (8)	167
Avier Jackson (8)	168
Oscar Hudgell (8)	169
Orson Sibley (7)	170
Hannah Francis (8)	171
Rosey Hawkins (8)	172
Isla Weston (7)	173
Ava-Rose Clark (7)	174

Isabella Thachter (8)	175
Zac Hewitt (8)	176
Freddie Rusbridge (8)	177
Seb Woodcock (8)	178
Millie Rawlinson (8)	179
Emilia Jayne Hall (7)	180
Savannah Brinck-Davis (7)	181
Nicole Susan Moore (8)	182
Sienna Morgan (8)	183

Rush Green Primary School, Romford

Danny Tooneear Kelly (7)	184
Tiago Roddrigues (8)	185

Sacred Heart Catholic Primary School, Ruislip

Reg Barrett (10) & Devon Moran	186

Saxon Primary School, Shepperton

Hollie Jessica Banister (11)	187
Isabelle Willoughby (10)	188
Vika Nekhaenko (10)	189
Lucy Taylor (11)	190
Chloe Palmer (11)	191
Alfie Sumer (11)	192
Logan Phillips (11)	193

St Cedd's CE (VA) Primary School, Bradwell On Sea

Amélie Shearer (11)	194
Kelsey E Loerns (11)	196
Chloe Guy (10)	197
Rhianna Richardson (10)	198
Thomas George (11)	199
Poppy Newby (10)	200
Cian Thomas (10)	201
Sian Eley (10)	202
Theo Brown (10)	203
Emma Tamar Lamb (11)	204

Jessie Lipscombe (10)   205
Dennis Cooch (10)   206

St Peters CE Primary School, South Weald

Harriet Olivia Dann (10)   207
Poppy Holder (9)   208
Eshan Jarvis (10)   209
Isabel Slaney (10)   210

St Teresa Catholic Primary School, Dagenham

Brielle Minta (8)   211
Lucas Cretu   212
Cherish Chiziterem O'kasi (7)   214
Toni Osoba (8)   215
Benas Taujanskas (8)   216
Toluwa Lateef (7)   217
Christine Kirumbi (8)   218
Marcela Gnaczynska   219
Courtney Chiagozikam O'kasi (7)   220
Teddy Benton (8)   221
Sophie Attard (7)   222
Marlena Gnaczynska (8)   223
Matthew Akinseye (8)   224

THE POEMS

Candy Land

C an you hear all the shouts and screams here?

A fter all, our land is all edible, so pop in if you are near,

N othing is not edible, just junk, bad for teeth,

D oors are made from marzipan,

Y es, come here if you can.

L ook and see our liquorice lakes

A nd the walls are made of chocolate cake,

N ot one thing costs a penny,

D o you now want to come?

Shifra Glickman (9)
Beis Chinuch Primary School, Edgware

The Good Dragon

The dragon as green as grass,
Just went to take his class
To learn how to fly
Throughout the night sky.

The moon quickly said,
"Don't come back dead."
But before the dragon could listen,
He was off in the sky with a glisten.

The dragon found food,
Who was puss in boots.
The dragon let him live,
As he was feeling positive.

The dragon got the title: the good dragon,
But it would always sadden
The other dragons,
Who thought this kind of thing could never
happen.

He became more friendly,
But he was still quite deadly

He flew off in the sky,
Without saying goodbye.

He flew onto a rock,
To look at the clock,
To see if it was time,
To have a great dine.

Demario Campbell (10)

Buxlow Preparatory School, Wembley

Superhero City

S neaking around the secret road,

U nderneath the glare of street lights,

P eeping around corners, looking for crime.

E very superhero is on duty at night,

R owing as fast as the Flashy across the sea!

H elping maidens in distress.

E veryone is sleeping soundly in bed.

R unning across the street to help...

O ther superheroes said it was their day off!

C atching baddies is a piece of cake!

I nside the Superhero HQ, they plan their escape.

T ogether they fight crime until dawn.

Y ou can be sure that you will be protected
wherever you are in Superhero City! Pow! Zap!
Pow! Zap! Pow! Zap!

Charles Kerley (9)
Buxlow Preparatory School, Wembley

Candy Land

Come to Candy Land where lollies are falling from the sky.
Come to Candy Land where rainbows are candyfloss.
Come to Candy Land where everything tastes sweet.
Come to Candy Land where the chocolate rivers flow through the town.
Come to Candy Land to enjoy the freshly picked toffees from the trees.
Come to see the beautiful and different colours of the buildings.
Come to Candy Land to enjoy the marvellous rain of slush.
Come to Candy Land where you'll find lollies growing beside the river.
Come to Candy Land where your dreams come true.

Shazeb Abbasi (9)
Buxlow Preparatory School, Wembley

Beatle Land

Welcome to Beatle Land!
The Beatles were a famous band.
Which consisted of four men, three played guitars
Named Lennon, Macca, Harrison and Starr.

In this land, you would have seen,
People travel by yellow submarine
And crossing Abbey Road, that's true,
One day that person could be you.

All of the land's boundaries
Are made of Beatley things
From album covers to posters galore
And a picture of Lucy and many more.

So come on now, take my hand
And we'll go together to Beatle Land.

Lilia Porter (10)
Buxlow Preparatory School, Wembley

Candy Island

C hocolate Smarties pebble the beach
A ll the trees are made up of sweets!
N ever believed such a place exists,
D airy milk pavements below our feet,
Y ummy lollipops ready to eat!

I ce cream for breakfast, lunch and tea,
S ugary sweets for you and for me,
L icking lemon and limey treats
A nd marshmallow cushions on our seats.
N iceties, novelties all you can eat,
D on't tell the adults we don't brush our teeth!

Sumeet Shah (9)
Buxlow Preparatory School, Wembley

Gemstone City

If you want to become rich,
visit Gemstone City.
Where everything is made of jewels,
so valuable and pretty!

If you're just popping in
just grab some dirt.
It's made of gold and silver,
which means you'll never have to work!

The most fabulous sight is the rainbow.
It is very precious to them,
ruby, topaz, diamond, emerald, sapphire and
amethyst,
made entirely out of gems.

Sia Dattani (10)
Buxlow Preparatory School, Wembley

Sports Land!

There is a beautiful land not full of sand,
It has the name of Sports Land.
It is full of people and full of joy
And was created by Ashab, a young boy!
The people who play in Sports Land are full of fun,
In the cricket they run,
In football they stun!
Sports Land, we all love it there,
We all play without a care.
It is a magical place where the sun never goes down,
It is a place where no one frowns.

Ashab Akbar (9)

Buxlow Preparatory School, Wembley

Topsy Turvy

T his land is ever so turbulent

O h my, it's upside down!

P art of me thinks this is a dream

S urely it is

Y et the rest of me is convinced it's reality

T here is no gravity here

U naccustomed to this monumental change

R eally difficult to take in

V ery perplexed, alone and scared

Y earning to be the right way round.

Yuv Dattani (10)
Buxlow Preparatory School, Wembley

The Island Of Flowers

The Island of Flowers,
Contains a brilliant amount of power,
Lots of rose flowers,
Dance in cocoa powder,
The powder is extremely sour,
The flowers became rotten in half an hour,
The horses that neigh,
Eat palm trees that sway,
But only the ones at the mysterious bay,
Funky gibbons laugh,
As they cross the gold-plated path,
And all the flowers say,
"Hey, go away!"

Raihan Ahmed (8)
Buxlow Preparatory School, Wembley

Toys Are Fun

T oys are fun to play with in Toy Land

O f course toys are fun

Y ou have toys. I have toys, we all have toys

S ome are wooden, some are metal, some are plastic

A lways with you

R emember the old times

E xpand your imagination

F orget the sad times

U nite with toys

N ever ever make you sad.

Div Mittal (11)

Buxlow Preparatory School, Wembley

I Dream

When I dream,
I dream of a tropical isolated island.
I dream of eating strawberries and cream,
I dream of relaxing on the sandy beach
And not thinking about school.
I dream of swimming in the water with tropical fish,
I dream of a car horn,
Oh no! This is not a dream,
I'm stuck in traffic on my way to school!

Amelia Khan (9)
Buxlow Preparatory School, Wembley

Super Slime World

Here in this world everything is made of slime,
You couldn't have it for a million dimes.
When it is sunny there's a rainbow,
That burns all the slime people's pupils.
The ground is gooey,
A place where the singing bird says, "Cooee!"
It is a beautiful bend
With no end.

Shona-Jasmine Patel (9)
Buxlow Preparatory School, Wembley

Lava Island

This island is an amazing sight!
It's made of lava and that is very strange.
I saw a coconut made of lava
But I thought it would burn my tongue.
Anyway I did not want to feel lava so I didn't set foot,
I stayed on my boat and sailed away
So I certainly did not play.

Paul Oladele (9)
Buxlow Preparatory School, Wembley

Art

My world is made of art,
It's so beautiful that my art can make you fart.
My land is so gorgeous you could call it blissful,
My paintings are as good as an apple tart,
My art is the opposite of disgraceful.

My world is full of vibrant colours,
They're better than all your sculptures.
I can make things pretty using pen and paper,
Even the most unsightly vulture.
I draw paintings that suit many cultures.
Now in my land there is a rupture,
It is exploding paint now I have to fly away in
departure,
Farewell my land,
I am taking my art in my cart.

Inaya Ahmed (7)
Cranford Primary School, Cranford

On Eid Day

C hildren open their gifts excitedly.

E verybody wears new, shiny and nice clothes.

L eave for Masjid early for prayers.

E ating sweet and yummy desserts.

B eautiful girls wearing bangles and henna.

R ead the Holy Quran.

A ll Muslims greet each other with joy!

T reating and looking after poor.

I nvite families for feast,

O ut to different places.

N ow the day has came to an end!

S ay Allah's name and thank Him for a lovely day.

Kashaf Khurram (7)

Cranford Primary School, Cranford

Candy World

My candy world is as colourful as a rainbow,
I see magical trees grow candy all over the place.
I taste the sticky and gooey gum in the big pink
yummy river.
I touch the cold and icy ice cream
and the soft marshmallow and pretty unicorn and
squishy corn.
I hear wafer houses cling and clang making silly
noises all over the place.
I smell strawberry candy canes sitting happily,
guarding the wafer houses from strangers.
I love my candy world!

Ryma Mekki (8)
Cranford Primary School, Cranford

Music Land

M y beautiful land is full of music.

U mbrellas are banned because it never rains.

S wearing is rude so you'll probably go to jail.

I t's so calm and peaceful in my world.

C ritically my world can't work without sunshine.

L oving as a mum and dad.

A lso caring as a grandparent.

N othing bad ever happens in Music Land.

D ogs are really popular and cute in this land.

Nihal Singh Bhatti (7)
Cranford Primary School, Cranford

What Music Is All About To You And Me

M elodies as beautiful as chocolate ice cream melting in your mouth on a summer's day!

U ndeniably the colourful sparkly disco lights have a glow like the light of love in the air!

S inging together loudly will wake up your tune! Bang! Pop! Fizz! Whizz!

I love music so do you! So let's make music for ever and ever.

C omfortable, calming and caring music will help you to do many good things!

Briti Malhan (7)
Cranford Primary School, Cranford

Happy Diwali!

D iwali Divas twinkling bright like a star,

I ndian festival to symbolise victory of good over evil,

W orship Lord Ganesha and goddess Lakshmi for peace and prosperity,

A dorning entrances with toran and rangoli designs,

L ots of delicious sweets, multicoloured cracking fireworks and gifts to share,

I n the darkest autumn night, it's a festival of light.

Aarav Sharma (8)

Cranford Primary School, Cranford

Candy Land

In Candy Land,
Stuff your hand,
With as much as you can,
You would never see a fat man.

Nor catch sight of bricks,
But you will see chocolate sticks,
Clouds made of cotton candy,
Sugar is perfect for a beach that is sandy.

Trees are now pink,
When you blink,
You see your dream,
Now mud is whipped cream.

Yummy, yummy in my tummy!

Arjun Varshney (7)
Cranford Primary School, Cranford

Piano World

P iano, my grand piano, perfect and peaceful,

I n this melodious land, music is always alive.

A lovely sight to behold, where music rocks and rolls,

N imble notes fall from the sky, they are just passing by,

O ver the hills and far away, my notes are going on a holiday.

S oon I will be there, feeling the musical air.

Ishant Bhaumik (8)

Cranford Primary School, Cranford

Candy Land

At Candy Land there are a lot of people with a
handful of sweets,
You can even get animals which you can actually
eat!
A funny cat with a yummy hat which loves to eat a
gummy rat.
You can even eat a lollipop tree then you'll feel
very free and get a lot of glee.
If you eat the candyfloss clouds you'll toss you
candy bag around!

Ranvitha Nagareddygari (8)
Cranford Primary School, Cranford

Music Land

My land is called Music,
It's calm and relaxing,
It feels as if you are hearing
The sound of the deep, blue sea.
It also feels like the sound
Of the calm breeze.
People come to hear
The beautiful sound
Of my music.
It has lots of instruments
Like drums and trumpets.

Ethan Lucas (7)
Cranford Primary School, Cranford

The Wonderful Candy Land

Made of sugar and spice
And all things nice
This island of sun
And all things fun

Deserts of desserts
Sugary trees
Ice cream so cold
You will get brain freeze

Jelly babies
And gummy bears
Gingerbread house
With gingerbread stairs.

Sarah Aliyah Mourandie (7)

Cranford Primary School, Cranford

The Land Of Sports Waits

The wondrous land of sports lies beyond infinity
The racquets of ping pong play by themselves
Waiting and waiting for someone to come
Cricket and football mix themselves
Playing cricket with a football and football with a
cricket ball
Again, waiting and waiting...

Jeeyaa Chettiar (8)
Cranford Primary School, Cranford

Gummy Land!

In Skittle City everything's pretty.
But in Gummy Land it's even better!
Bounce everywhere and snack all day.
Purple or pink, whatever you think,
It doesn't matter,
Each way every day.
Gummies in my tummy,
Taste very yummy!
Gummy!

Sharan Kang (8)
Cranford Primary School, Cranford

My Magnificent World

D ad brought me plenty of fireworks.

I was with my mum, dad and friends.

W hat a wonderful night we had.

A lso we had a lovely home-made food.

L ater we went bowling for fun.

I was very, very excited to see the fireworks.

Medha Ramagiri (8)

Cranford Primary School, Cranford

Candy Land

C ome to a land where there is so much sticky, sugary sand,

A world filled with candy that you'll love,

N o houses stand without candy,

D oors made out of caramel trees,

Y ou would love it, so land in this wondrous world.

Aqeel Fazal (7)
Cranford Primary School, Cranford

Candy City

C olourful Candy City sounds so nice.

A s tasty as toffee, it scares away the mice.

N owhere in the world could this be seen.

D iving in the chocolate river with Dean.

Y ummy, yummy in my tummy.

Chitleen (7)

Cranford Primary School, Cranford

Nightmare Town!

Nightmare Town has ghosts that will attack.
But you can never go back.
Only a fool wouldn't be afraid of this place!
Where all gross ghouls live and give life then make death!
Nightmare Town is like a scare fair!

Jamal Sherman (8)
Cranford Primary School, Cranford

Candy Unicorns

C olossal candyfloss clouds, floating across the sky.

A stonishing skittles and M&Ms fall from the sky as rain.

N eat, soft beds appear as soon as you yawn.

D azzling stars glisten and twinkle while you fall asleep.

Y odel and sing because no one can stop you.

U ltimate kindness and respect will be given to you.

N ominate yourself and others because awards are there.

I mpeccable food is created for you to savour.

C arefully bubblegum unicorns carry you safely.

O btain wings and a horn and become a 'fairycorn'!

R adiant and jolly are all qualities here,

N ow come and join!

S leep peacefully under colourful rainbows!

Eliza Costas (10)

Glade Primary School, Clayhall

Candy Land

Candy Land is a beautiful land,
Where everything is made of candy and sweet sands.
It is not only beautiful but it is also a wonderland.

Here the grasses are made of green, bouncy, jiggly jelly,
Which is really so delicious,
Which I am sure will surpass everyone's imaginations.

The trees are brown with leaves made of cream.
The fruits, even when they are ripe, are green.
The houses are made of chocolate bricks,
The jelly and caramel makes them stick.
The clouds and the sky are respectively made of white and blue cotton candy.

The patches of the clouds glide away across the sky gently,
The animals are made of gummies and milk chocolate

and they are running around everywhere,
So it is not very difficult,
If you wish you can find them anytime, anywhere.

And there is always a light background music
and a mild scented breeze is blowing back and
forth,
It is really a heaven on Earth.

Nilufer Yasmin Alam (7)
Glade Primary School, Clayhall

...But No Chocolate

Popping out of triangular plants,
Candy canes, swaying in the sweet breeze,
...But no chocolate

All different sizes and colours,
The lollipop trees reach mountain height,
They are everywhere you go,
Near where the syrup river flows,
...But no chocolate

Plunged in the depths of the grass,
The jelly bean rocks lie,
As the sweet scent will spray,
...But no chocolate

Buzzing above the trees and plants,
The sweet bugs dance,
...But no chocolate.

Everywhere you look gummy people run,
They will come and greet you so you have fun.

But deep underground past tunnels and vines,
Sits the chocolate monster hogging all the
chocolate with pride,
In the corner of his hole was the chocolate tied,
So now we know,
That's where the chocolate lies.

Krishan Patel (10)
Glade Primary School, Clayhall

Winter Wonderland

A place of wonder and desire,
A place that is filled with dreams,
It is like I'm on my very own team!
That snow feels all squishy to me,
Don't you see?

What are you waiting for, come along.
Inside is a magical surprise waiting,
Never miss the free offer of coming,
Try out the ride, well I should say sweet!
Everything in this city is very, very pretty,
Rate this place five stars, I know it!

Every December it is winter!
I see snow falling from the sky,
I also see trees swishing right to left,
To right, back again, jabbing really rustly,
I can hear wind,
Breathing wind.

I can taste the snowflakes on my tongue,
I can feel the pointy leaves on the snowy trees,
I smell the wind blowing all over the place,
I love...
Winter Wonderland.

Zulekha Khan
Glade Primary School, Clayhall

Long Lost Treasure

Off we sail,
On the turbulent seas.
Our ship's called the 'The Rusty Nail',
Searching for gold that reaches your knees.
The Forbidden Land we reach at dawn,
I wake up fast with a long slow yawn.
With our spades we dig up the treasure chest,
Finding diamonds and rubies we take a rest.

"Ahoy me sailors, let's go home."
"Tomorrow, we'll be rich and as happy as a
gnome!"
Next time join us if you can,
You won't regret it, you'll become a fan!
But when we all came to plunder our gold,
To buy all the things that we couldn't afford.
We discovered that the Captain had gone aboard,
And with him had gone all our hoard!

Zak Abbas Ahmed (9)
Glade Primary School, Clayhall

Nightmare Land

This is the place of nightmares,
Where you don't dare to pick your hairs.
Everything is not fine,
Although the clock gives a great big chime,
The grass in the land is very dark,
You can't even make light spark.
There are terrifying creatures there,
In fact they might be everywhere.
You're not going to have dinner,
Because there is no winner.
The water there is cursed,
Don't drink it otherwise you will get worse.
The windows are shattered,
It could make your teeth chatter.
In this place there is wind,
But you don't know what is about to begin,
So if you dare to come to this land,
Good luck will bring you a chopped hand.

Faaez Sheikh (10)
Glade Primary School, Clayhall

Odd City

In this city it is very, very odd,
Also in the city everything is pretty,
with tasty chocolate logs,
There are lovely bogs with frogs
and everyone has to eat cod.
There's a room filled with crazy cats,
Another room with flying mats,
Including dogs with baseball bats!
And old grannies that always chat!

There are flying unicorns that shoot candyfloss
And in this city I am the boss!
So in the football matches there is no loss.

There are lots of different shapes.
That you can make.
You can even bake a chocolate cake.
Visit soon and you can have a band loom.
Whilst listening to your favourite tune.

Sasha Brumand Francis (9)
Glade Primary School, Clayhall

Dreams Or Nightmares

Nightmares, are places for your mind to explore,
Dreams and nightmares make your life so much more.
Scary ghosts jump from behind a lamp post,
While superheroes catch those who boast.
Some kids dream about a sidekick hamster in town,
Others dream of scary clowns.
Scary noises in the night,
Make tiny creatures give you a fright.
Magical mermaids save you from danger,
Whilst peaceful babies lie in their manger.
Some people dream of a land made of candy,
Some people dream of a skeleton called Mandy.
Sleep tight knowing when you wake up,
Everything will be alright.

Saara Naiem Dakri (10)
Glade Primary School, Clayhall

Candy Life

I climb the vines to avoid the river of slime,
It has an amazing shine.
The jungle birds are no match for the herds of
velociraptors below,
I shoot a bow and arrow like a pro.

Gummy bears have funky hair,
They even have a crazy stare,
They hum to the beat of the drum.
Scurry of rats can be heard by the bats,
As they run through the jungle caves.

A volcano spills out lava made of jelly bean goo,
This whole island looks like a crazy zoo!
Mighty dinosaurs are big, bad brutes,
All the other animals are in cahoots.

Zachary Sheikh (10)
Glade Primary School, Clayhall

The Greenhill Zone

In the Greenhill Zone...
A confused cheetah chased a creeping caterpillar
through the loop the loop.
A mischievous monkey managed to mount the
wobbly wall and slide down.
A happy hedgehog hopped on the huge trampoline
and landed in a tree.

A coconut fell from the tree,
It landed on the cheetah's tail,
The cheetah screamed ever so loudly,
The monkey heard and started laughing.
The hedgehog fell off the tree,
The cheetah saw and began to giggle,
The hedgehog joined in and they all laughed
happily ever after.

Ashvin Muhilazhagan (8)
Glade Primary School, Clayhall

Bookmark Maze

In Bookmark Maze,
Life's a daze,
Lost in a book,
Locked in every cranny and nook.

In Bookmark Maze,
Life's a daze
Living in a dream
Not a drop of dread.

In Bookmark Maze,
Life's a daze,
You never know where you may venture,
Though you know it's an adventure.

In Bookmark Maze,
It's a daze,
You never want to leave it,
Never want to stop,
Reading, reading till your brain goes... *Pop!*
Then it's time for your... Bookmark!

Maria Imaan Akter (10)
Glade Primary School, Clayhall

Milkshake Mania!

In Milkshake Mania,
Everything is sweet,
Milkshake mountains loom over cream and sugar
valleys,
Joy is everywhere,
There isn't one vegetable,
But with fruits it's another story,
Melon mountains, strawberry homes,
Apple animals and more,

Rivers of milk and sugar trees,
There's not one speck of veg or leaves,
The world is round and tangerine like an orange,
The ground is edible and is a mixture of various
fruits,
Caramel sticks it together,
Making it sticky like glue!

Ayaan Jalil (9)
Glade Primary School, Clayhall

The Winterlands

W interlands is the place I like to be.

I n my land streams run free.

N othing is there but snow and ice.

T here are wonderful creatures big and small.

E veryone's welcome in my land of joy.

R abbits run free throughout my land.

L et everyone come and have plenty of fun.

A ll are welcome to my wonderful kingdom.

N othing can stop us from having fun.

D ecember is the best time of year.

S now never melts and the fun never ends.

Christopher Grieff (9)

Glade Primary School, Clayhall

Maryland

In yummy Candy Land
The brown trees are
Filled with chocolate keys
and candy cream

Our magical rivers are
made of cookie cream
The floating clouds are
Soft, soft candyfloss

Houses are made of cupcakes
The bricks of the houses are
made of marshmallows

The pointy mountains are
Made of Toblerone
Yummy caramel fills
every stone

Sun in Maryland
always reminds me
of Ferrero Rocher
I love my land because of Maryland.

Ashwika Mishra (7)
Glade Primary School, Clayhall

My Secret Garden

My secret garden,
It says I am ardent,
Birds tweeting, everyone's busy weeding
Plants, that make everyone dance,
Flowerpots, make colourful dots,
The sun's job is done,
The trampoline, looks like an eager teen,
The playhouse, makes your dream day house,
Woe, the shed is dead.
Rattling, rattling, everything's scattering,
The fence is brown like it's down,
My secret garden, says I am ardent,
It's a beautiful day.

Adam Haq (8)
Glade Primary School, Clayhall

Dream Land

We have hearts on go-carts
Sandy, pink sand all in our own Dream Land
We have magical jewellery for the girls
We have flying cars for the boys
All on sale
Without a penny to spend
You will not even have to lend
Can't you see
That it's free
We have sparkly phones
This is where nobody moans
Everyone can fly
You will never sigh
We have it all here in Dream Land
(By the way, no one ever gets stranded at Dream
Land).

Jandice Stewart (9)
Glade Primary School, Clayhall

Candy World

Candy helps me study,
Candy makes me hyper
And it makes me jump off my feet.
Candy is sour and sweet.
It's so good to eat,
When it's on the floor,
It may start to stink.
It's my favourite thing to eat,
Candy canes, lollipops, candy bars and more,
If you eat all of the candy your teeth will become
sore,
Candy is so sweet,
It's a great treat,
I think candy is bubblelicious,
and it will be delicious!

Alice Costan (9)
Glade Primary School, Clayhall

Yummy Land!

In my land everything is yummy,
There is not a treat that doesn't fill your tummy!
Nothing is sickeningly sweet,
You'll find everything here is a treat!

There are chocolate lakes,
Everything is edible, nothing is fake.
The houses are made of ginger
And so are their games like Jenga.

The sand is yellow like corn,
The sky is pink like marshmallows at dawn.
Everything is yummy,
It's a treat for your tummy.

Zara Islam (10)
Glade Primary School, Clayhall

Tolerant Town

In Tolerant Town everybody's friends,
There's no one who's mean,
There's no one who is friendless,
The only things you see are...
Nice people,
Helping the poor,
Selling bread,
And of course making a new friend!
Bullies are not tolerated!
Only if it was the same...
Everywhere!
Treating others big and small nicely.
Then our world could be a better place
Because in Tolerant Town
We are all friends.

Jedidiah Fadiora (10)
Glade Primary School, Clayhall

Peace City

Down in Peace City,
Everything is pleasant and pretty,
It's always peaceful and calm,
Though you might need to set your morning alarm.

Peace flowers do exist,
But the peace chocolate is hard to resist,
Everyone lives a stress-free life,
Not a speck of strife.

People are treated equally,
So everyone can live peacefully,
Peace City is really the place to be,
Come live peacefully just like me.

Myleesha Khaleeq (10)
Glade Primary School, Clayhall

The Circus Nightmare!

The clown will never frown,
It will always face down.
It follows you through the whole town,
Until you drown in the river beneath the ground.

Coming closer are the deadly ducks,
These will never cluck.
But they are very fond,
Of killing in your neighbour's pond!

Please don't go to this circus,
Or you will die.
Then the bats will pick you up and fly,
For now stay outside the circus.

Amrit Kaur Uppal (10)
Glade Primary School, Clayhall

Unikitty Island

The scent of sugar fills the land,
Not anything here will ever be bland,
Candy canes are everywhere,
Look at the forest of lollipops there!

Kitties in that corner,
Unicorns in the other,
Together there are more,
Unikitties galore!

Feel their soft fur,
Then listen to their purr,
Join the party,
There's always a big malarkey!

Unikitty, Unikitty, Unikitty Island!

Maryam Loonat (9)
Glade Primary School, Clayhall

Snow Land

Snow, snow, everywhere,
flakes gliding into my hair.
My foot goes in and is hard to drag out,
I pull it free with a little shout.

The trees stood tall and proud.
The snow from the branches falls down to the ground.
Animals shelter from the winter's snow,
searching for somewhere warm to go.

Children wrap up warm to play outdoors.
Looking to the rooftops for their hero, Santa Claus!

Daniel Walters (10)
Glade Primary School, Clayhall

All The Magic Things

A fairy reaches up so high
With a twinkle in her eye
To place a star in the sky
So all the fairies will stop to cry.

On the beach where the children play
A little mermaid stays in the bay
Feeling sad that she can't be part
Of the fun that has just begun.

I see a dragon in the sky
With a wing that can really fly
Oh how I wish I could be there
To see the wonderful affair.

Milea Deysel (9)
Glade Primary School, Clayhall

Magical Unicorns

U nicorns play in the magical forest of Unicornia,

N aughty unicorns play late into the night,

I magination is without limits in Unicornia,

C ome and join in with the fun to be had,

O cean breeze is so wonderful and refreshing,

R iding unicorns is the most fantastic thing,

N eat and tidy unicorns are beautiful creatures,

S pectacular are unicorns in Unicornia.

Vanessa Patel (7)
Glade Primary School, Clayhall

Football Fantasy

In Football Fantasy you can score top bins,
And that will lead to plenty of wins.
In Football Fantasy I hear kids laughing,
While the adults are photographing.
We play fun games, that's no joke
But before we do that we have to drink Coke.
In this world you can drive *tanks*,
But your name has to be Frank.
Everyone supports the same team
But I can't say the same about live streams.

Kaiden Small (10)
Glade Primary School, Clayhall

Fairy-Tale Land

Where briars bloom
And there isn't any gloom,
People laugh, sleep and play during the day.
Glass slippers and lots of apples,
Have been enchanted by the evil cackles,
A magic palace lies on the cloud,
Where lots of people sing aloud.
Fairies are dancing in midair,
While people are eating chocolate eclairs.
The big bad wolf gave a puff
But Little Red Riding Hood said that's enough.

Jannath Islam (10)
Glade Primary School, Clayhall

Gummy Land

Gummy Land is sweet,
There's no such thing as a beat,
Gummy Land can sing,
And you can wear bling.
In Gummy Land if you jump,
You won't get a bump.
In Gummy Land cats pounce,
Whilst you can bounce.
If you jump house to house,
You have to wear a blouse.
You can eat,
Whilst sitting in a gummy seat.
You can drink out of a gummy glass,
And in all tests you will pass!

Aliyah Jones (10)
Glade Primary School, Clayhall

Gummy Land

Everything here looks so yummy,
Won't you just try some gummy.
It's just like heaven,
Don't you feel like you're seven?

In here it's so pretty,
Don't you think this is a nice city?
It's so colourful,
That you will never feel awful.

Just look at the cola,
It kind of sounds like Crayola.
It's so fizzy,
That it will make you busy.

Zahra Amir (9)
Glade Primary School, Clayhall

Gaming World

From Mario to Bowser,
From PS4 to Wii U,
You can do whatever you can,
While eating bacon, cheese and ham.

Gaming in, gaming out,
What else could you do?
In Gaming World.

From Super Mario to Mario Kart,
From Sonic to Spider-Man,
Which is the best?
In gaming world.

Gaming in, gaming out,
What else could you do?
In Gaming World.

Sahib Singh Sond
Glade Primary School, Clayhall

Candy Cane! Candy Cane Land!

Candy Cane Land!
Candy Cane Land!
What a treat,
Ever so sweet!
They hang from trees
And smile with glee!
Candy Cane Land!
Candy Cane Land!
It tastes very good,
Just like it should!
No bricks,
Just candy cane sticks!
Candy Cane Land!
Candy Cane Land!
It's still green,
All made of cream!
In Candy Cane Land!
Candy Cane Land!

Kayan Zorba (9)
Glade Primary School, Clayhall

Aloo Loompa Land!

In Aloo Loompa Land nothing is bland!
You will be spaced with a taste of cumin,
chilli and coriander,
So there will be no room for a bystander.

Paratha shaped, round and browned,
Thin as if it had been rolling pinned out.

Aloo Loompas are tall potato creatures,
That are in charge of all the features,
As they are the keepers!

Yashika Pandey (10)
Glade Primary School, Clayhall

Candy Land

Candy Land,
Candy Land,
Candy Land,
Everything is sweet.
The smell will whisk you off your feet.
The gummy bear shops
Will be your first stop
And don't forget the park
But please don't eat the chocolate tree bark
And our biscuity sand
Will flow through your hand,
Candy Land,
Candy Land,
Candy Land.

Ava Dhadwal (7)
Glade Primary School, Clayhall

Dinosaurs On Snow And Ice

The sky is blue,
The sea is ice,
Everyone says it's true,
Because it's cold and everyone's nice.

The igloos are frozen,
All you can see is white.
There are about a dozen
Dinosaurs in sight.

The trees are swaying,
The wind is blowing.
The children are playing,
The dinosaurs are growling.

Ayaan Ahmed (9)
Glade Primary School, Clayhall

Happy Land

In Happy Land,
Everything is grand,
From the mountains of snow,
You can watch the dragons go,

In the underwater caves,
You can see the mermaids,
Swim up to where it's sunny,
To see their pet bunnies,

The magical bunnies can fly,
High up in the sky,
It is so bright,
In the sunlight.

Connie May Shell (7)
Glade Primary School, Clayhall

Candy Land

My home is made of candy
Our homes are very handy
We eat all day
And dream away
We go to work
Here, no darkness will lurk
We love to eat
Oh, it's so sweet!

Here in Candy Land
We always love to give a hand
There are no police, laws or rules
Only chocolate filled swimming pools.

Vikram Singh (10)
Glade Primary School, Clayhall

A Friend

A friend,
There's nothing like a good friend,
You're always there for me,
When I need you the most,
A friend is someone to laugh with,
Or someone to cry with,
A true friendship lasts a lifetime,
A friendship is strong,
The strongest in the world,
And no one can ruin it.
A friend.

Archie Batts (10)
Glade Primary School, Clayhall

Candy Land

Come with me and you shall see Candy Land,
As beautiful as can be.
With rocks as soft as pillows,
You can eat them because they're marshmallows.
It's pretty and it's colourful,
With a giant chocolate waterfall.
It's delicious and it's yummy,
It's enough to fill your tummy.

Madison Roundacre (7)
Glade Primary School, Clayhall

GD City!

G reat creators roam the streets,
D angerous hackers hide in dark corners,

C razy levels appear everywhere,
I ncredible players roam the demon level house,
T alented YouTubers film all the time,
Y uril, Surv, Riot, FunnyGame are just some of the famous people.

Luke Moore (10)
Glade Primary School, Clayhall

Candy World

In Candy World it is very sweet,
So good, it's good enough to eat,
Cotton candy trees,
Haribo people, cookie rocks,
String with candy used as necklaces,
Chewy sweets used as leaves,
Sugar rain,
So tasty and delicious,
But they're not vicious,
And very ambitious for candy.

Donnell Lemar Lucky-Oligie
Glade Primary School, Clayhall

Maze Land

In the land of maze,
We hide and chase,
We go on adventures,
Searching for exciting ventures,
We look for ways,
To exit our maze,
Apart from our labyrinth,
There's a river you can swim in,
There are green hedges,
All over the labyrinth's edges.

Amber Starling (9)
Glade Primary School, Clayhall

My Bed Is Like A Car

My bed is like a car,
When I am tucked in,
I take a trip to the road,
Drive to places far away.

I drive past the trees,
I heard the pop music
At the top of the stage.

I am back in bed,
My car drives at night,
Comes home at morning light.

Shasvathan Uthayakumaran (9)
Glade Primary School, Clayhall

Ice Cream Land

Ice cream here,
Ice cream there,
Ice cream land has ice cream everywhere.

Put it on cake,
Put it on fruit,
But most of all I like it with chocolate sauce.

It is so sweet,
It is so tasty,
I am never going home
Or leaving ice cream city.

Danyaal Ahmed (9)
Glade Primary School, Clayhall

Car Crazy

Cars are really cool,
Heavy and reliable.
Every single one,
Mercedes to Bugatti.
You can race with all your might,
The cars are a great sight.
Mercedes as the moon.
Suzuki as the sun.
This world is different,
Undeniably brilliant.

Jayden Gable Williams (10)
Glade Primary School, Clayhall

Loopty Land

"Roar!" the dinosaurs say,
and the unicorns go neigh,
The rocket goes *boom*
and heads to the moon.
The castle has knights
and has epic fights.
There are superheroes galore
and rabbits that gnaw.

Jack Grimsey (9)
Glade Primary School, Clayhall

Fruit Land

F ind a tree to eat some fruit,

R oots help a fruit grow,

U gni is a beautiful berry,

I t is healthy and worth picking,

T ake a fruit, it won't shoot. Have fun eating your fruit!

Ruth Anne Leonce (8)

Glade Primary School, Clayhall

The Heroic Team

H eroes are protectors,
E ach one is famous,
R ighteousness as a hero,
O ne hero is in each country,
I n each country heroes have different fame,
C an also be together.

Maanav Aravindan

Glade Primary School, Clayhall

Candy Land

Candy Land is an amazing place,
The trees of candy canes,
Fresh chocolate from the warm chocolate river,
The fluffy sweet grass,
Chocolate people that you can eat.

Riti Limani (7)
Glade Primary School, Clayhall

Harry Potter Land

H at with history chose my house,
A rat that really isn't really a mouse.
R avenclaw, Gryffindor, Hufflepuff and Slytherin,
R owing to Hogwarts,
Y ou'll hope your witches don't get warts.

P ottermore is our site,
O h, Voldemort is as scary as a snake.
T aught the best of Wizardry.
T rample on Miss Norris, leave in thirty.
E very wizard taught the best,
R on Weasley's hair ginger as an orange.

L ord Voldemort is out for Potter,
A lbus Dumbledore protects Harry forever.
N eville Longbottom is as scared as a mouse,
D umbledore, McGonagall, Snape and Filch.

Jessica O'Rourke (8)
Graham James Primary School, Corringham

Land Of All Lands

L and Of Mountains, they're bigger than big.

A Land Of Fun is very fun, you can play every day.

N o bit of wood in Candy Land, instead everything tastes good.

D ino Land is very dangerous, be careful!

O ff to Sand Land, very sandy, you go with Mandy.

F irst of the lands is Dino Land.

A ll of the lands are so pretty.

L ands, so many lands.

L ove Land is where you go for love.

L and Of All Lands is very fun

A nd at the end you sadly have to go home.

N ow the next day you have more fun, fun, fun.

D own in the lands you can have so much fun,

S andy Land is full of candy.

Vinnie Turner (8)

Graham James Primary School, Corringham

Minecraft Land

M y friend and I were playing Minecraft

I have been sucked into the game

N o way, I have built a house out of green wooden blocks

E vil devils come at night and the Loch Ness Monster comes out

C raft a sword at the carpenters

R eally wish I lived in Minecraft Land

A pig is really square in Minecraft

F inally I got to explore Minecraft Land

T immy the chicken lives at Minecraft Land

L eather armour is easy to make

A pples can be red, golden and enchanted

N obody knows where my house is

D emi devils can't find me in my house. Mostly they can knock my door down.

Tommy Lewis Spears (8)

Graham James Primary School, Corringham

Candy Land

Candy Land is very yummy,
It feels funny in my tummy.
All the houses are made of sweets
And the river is melted by the heat.
With a popping candy bridge, that pops all day.
When you go to bed you lay.
The trees are made of gummy bears,
Sometimes there are even hares.
The grass is made of liquorice,
And it is very ticklish!
It rains Skittles and Smarties
And every night we party.
The unicorns are as white as snow,
They make cookies out of dough.
Candy Land is very fun,
Of course there is gum!
Candy Land is very sweet
You will always hear a beat.
The clouds are made of candyfloss,
And a Jelly Baby is the boss.

Emily Kench (7)
Graham James Primary School, Corringham

Land Of Food

Land Of Food is a great place to be,
There are no sorts of veg, not even a pea,
The healthy food has been banished,
Everything is edible,
It is despicable,
When you eat it, it grows back,
Even the trees you can eat,
Beware of the big burger beat,
It rains Coca-Cola Zero Sugar,
The big burger is very greedy,
He sometimes is a bit weedy,
The pizza is very strong,
When you roll him, he gets long,
The rain is as tasty as a burger,
There is absolutely no murder,
The floor is made out of pizza,
You might meet a girl called Lisa,
The trees grow chocolate,
Everyone is strange,
Because they work at the range.

Adam Bassett (7)
Graham James Primary School, Corringham

Future Land

F uture Land is cool,
U nder the school there is a secret hall.
T all buildings and people going to work,
U nconscious people by a man called 'Smurce',
R emaking mechanisms,
E veryday in the shop, people buy organisms.

L ady robots are fancy,
A nd a man called Ancy,
N o crossovers today,
D ays are fun in this place.

Alfie Henry (7)
Graham James Primary School, Corringham

Marshmallow

M arshmallow Land is very yummy, it makes my tummy very funny,

A t Marshmallow Land the river is very gooey,

R ich people can only go to Marshmallow Land.

S leeping in Marshmallow Land can be hard,

H otels are £1,002 to go in.

M arshmallow Land is weird and crazy,

A t Marshmallow Land you cannot get to sleep,

L eaning on the famous marshmallow wall you will get kicked out.

L earning in Marshmallow Land is very fun.

O utside in Marshmallow Land you can do anything.

W hen you are in Marshmallow Land you can do anything.

Bobby Long (8)

Graham James Primary School, Corringham

Dinosaur Land

D inosaurs are dangerous things.

I n the city we fight back.

N ight-time comes and they all disappear.

O ver the hills there are scary raptors attacking.

S ome baby dinosaurs are robots.

A llosauruses were chasing people.

U nder the ground there is an egg.

R ight underground their babies lay eggs.

L ands are actually good except this land.

A nd we want to move land to land.

N o people have had a baby yet.

D inos are not silly, they are killing machines.

Tyler Thomas Oakley (7)

Graham James Primary School, Corringham

Pirates At Sea

It's rough at sea
Most of the time for tea they have peas
The pirate ship is very big
It's bigger than a pig
In the middle of the ocean
There is an island for a pirate potion
Try not to make an explosion
Otherwise you'll wake Captain Hook
But the boat shook
So the pirate in the nest shouted, "Look out!"
There is a pig with a really long snout.
The pirates screamed, "Aargh, would you look at that."
That pig is extra fat
It looks like a nice piece of bacon
I wonder if it's taken!

Millie Farmer (7)
Graham James Primary School, Corringham

Game Land

P laying PlayStation is fun
L ego is an amazing game
A stud is worth 20 pounds
Y es, I like PlayStation
S unny every day
T ank games are fun
A zombie game is fun
T ank games have a lot of guns
I play games every day
O n most games there are guns
N ew games are fun

L ego Avengers is fun
A game with guns is fun
N ew things with new games are really fun
D inosaur games are very fun.

Regan Branch (7)
Graham James Primary School, Corringham

YoungWriters

Chocolate City

C hocolate is yummy for my tummy,

H arry is my brother, like a mummy,

O ver the land there is some chocolate,

C hocolate for my chocolatey stomach,

O h look at all that chocolate

L ike it every second of the day,

A nd it is so fun,

T he day is never done,

E very day I have a bit of chocolate.

C hocolate is very yummy,

I love Chocolate City,

T he city is the best of all

Y ou and me at Chocolate City.

Ellie-May Mannion (7)

Graham James Primary School, Corringham

Underwater Land

U nderwater Land is so fun

N ever a day without a run

D eep, deep down lived a little fish

E very fish made a splash

R eefs are so colourful

W here are all the fish?

A fter a go on the slide

T ime to dive

E very day I arrive

R eefs are exciting

L ots of games to be played

A ndy the fisherman played safely

N ets are good as they can catch fish

D eep down is more fun.

Callum Anderson (8)
Graham James Primary School, Corringham

M&M Land

M &M Land is colourful and everything's made from coated chocolate

A t 3am, the biggest M&M ever seen
N uts are the land walkers
D ark in the forest was a chocolate monster

M onsters are covered with caramel and chocolate

L andmarks are chocolate
A nd in the morning, the tables are just one
N ibble M&Ms all day
D ifferent flavoured M&Ms fall from the sky.

Bobby Iceton (7)

Graham James Primary School, Corringham

Pirates At Sea

P irates are very nasty

I heard of a captain with a hook

R um is what pirates drink

A rr that's what pirates say

T ie him to the wall or walk the plank

E dible creatures, that's what they eat

L ooking for a pirate lost out at sea

A t Pirate Land there is lots of treasure and dinner

N o girls they say, "Unless they're cool."

D irt and mess on the deck.

Lily Conquest (7)

Graham James Primary School, Corringham

Halloween

H alloween Land is dark and eerie.

A t night the graveyard comes to life.

L ate at night, at 3am, the lakes turn green.

L ots of people are scared at night.

O n Saturday ghosts are friendly instead of nasty.

W hen it's night, ghosts haunt your house.

E vil witches kill people.

E veryone should visit Halloween Land because it's spooky.

N ever walk through the graveyard on your own!

Aiden Kercher (7)
Graham James Primary School, Corringham

Halloween Land

H alloween Land is dark and scary

A nd is home to Scary Mary.

L ost in the forest at night,

L isten carefully, you don't want a fight.

O ld Vampire Rick is as dead as a stick.

W hen it's midnight everyone runs with a fright,

E veryone is scared because a wolf could bite.

E njoy your stay, you won't want to stay again,

N ext time you'll turn into a hen.

Thomas Vallis (8)

Graham James Primary School, Corringham

Mega Structure City

In Mega Structure City,
It's extremely pretty,
Buckingham palace to Sydney Opera House,
In the engines of Big Ben I see a mouse.

Mega Structure City, oh so sunny,
When you get there you would hop like a bunny,
Everyone's happy
And oh-so clappy.

The city's so sweet,
You would love to dance to the beat,
It's exciting and extremely magical,
And it's never, ever tragical!

Bethany Moore (8)
Graham James Primary School, Corringham

Underwater World

U nder the water is very dangerous

N ow there is a submarine near you

D eadly sharks swimming around

E very one of your friends will be there

R ushing waves can make the fish go away

W ater is very dangerous in the sea

A nd a whale swam above us

T oday we are going into the sea

E very day we see lots of sharks

R eally scary down here, isn't it.

James Baker (8)

Graham James Primary School, Corringham

Unicorn Land

U p in Unicorn Land there is a unicorn called Mandy,

N o, she does not have any candy,

I n this place there is fun,

C utting the tail is a job for Mum,

O n the fluffy cosy clouds,

R ain is very loud,

N ot the main thing,

L ambs are getting trained,

A nd they are never afraid,

N o, unicorns are not red,

D illan go to bed!

Callie Strong (8)

Graham James Primary School, Corringham

Wonder Land

W onder in my land
O n the way grab some candy by your hand
N o one can live at my place
D o not come into my base
E veryone's welcome to stay and stuff their face
R eady for the cookie race.

L earn the race
A nd don't forget the chocolate mountain
N ow everyone is allowed to eat my fountain
D o anything and keep chatting.

Archy Frogley (7)
Graham James Primary School, Corringham

Candy Land

C andy Land is very yummy
A t Candy Land you get lots of chocolate
N ice chocolate ice cream you can eat
D own in Candy Land jungle you will meet a lion
Y ou can see and eat candy.

L ater it is raining candyfloss
A pple pie with a top made of candy
N ever ever eat caramel because it might be sour
D rink chocolate in a popping candy castle.

Nevaeh Collier (7)
Graham James Primary School, Corringham

Dream Land

D ream Land is very friendly.

R eading is very fun.

E very night I dream of sweets.

A t night I watched the shooting stars.

M y land is very pretty and chocolatey.

L ate at night my bed turned into a gummy bed.

A t Dream Land there are fluffy cotton candy clouds.

N ext for breakfast I had a gummy worm.

D ream Land is beautiful and pretty.

Sian Donnelly (7)

Graham James Primary School, Corringham

Science Land

S cience Land is a great place,
C arefully people pack their cases,
I decide to fly,
E ven when I'm going high,
N o more flying for the day,
C hemicals are not allowed today,
E xperiments are fun,

L earning about the sun,
A bout today: it was great,
N o more running about,
D on't mess up my lab! Get out!

Tallulah Wevers (7)

Graham James Primary School, Corringham

Love Land

L ove Land is very warm and pink.

O n top of the mansion lives the Queen of Hearts.

V ery far away live our dark enemies.

E veryone is extremely happy.

L ate at night the Queen of Hearts turns into a giraffe.

A ll around the land, flow red heart rivers.

N ear the rivers is a beautiful princess' castle.

D eep in the river lives a mermaid.

Rosie-Jane Bateman (7)

Graham James Primary School, Corringham

Unicorn Land

U nicorns are great,
N ot one has been late.
I n the Candy Garden,
C andy, my friend, said pardon.
O ne of the dreams is mine,
R hyming takes time.
N ever forget Unicorn Land.

L ate or not magic is in my hand
A nd when you get home,
N ever forget you're not alone.
D id you have fun in Unicorn Land?

Emma Grace Laybourn (8)
Graham James Primary School, Corringham

Wonder City

W onder City it is so magical,

O n the way to Wonder City you will have a great day,

N o smugglers allowed in May,

D o have a good and crazy day,

E very day's easy-peasy,

R ead books every day,

C ome and see my world,

I n Wonder City it is so beautiful,

T he trees are so yummy,

Y ou will like Wonder City.

Amy Horncastle (8)

Graham James Primary School, Corringham

Mine Land

M ine Land is scary and dark

I 'm so scared because there are zombies at night

N ight and I'm in fright

E at as I walk down the street

L ights switching on and off

A s I look around a bunch of zombies come this way

N asty monsters chasing me around the street

D ead skeletons chasing me while I dig deep down.

Lewis Daniel Hatchett (8)

Graham James Primary School, Corringham

Candy Land

C andy Land sweets are so yummy
A nd I'm going to put some in my tummy
N o one knows where Candy Land is
D o you love Candy Land more than me?
Y ou can stuff your face all day

L ollipops are so delicious
A nd candy canes too
N o one loves candy more than I do
D reams at Candy Land always come true.

Ellsie Webb (7)

Graham James Primary School, Corringham

Diamond Land

Diamond Land is very clean,
But the city is very mean.
There is a diamond river,
Where the diamond snakes slither.
Next to the legendary diamond tree,
There is a legendary diamond bee.
Over the river of diamond sticks,
You will find a diamond castle,
Inside is the wise man: Nick.
Diamond games are so much fun,
If you want you can have a run.

Christopher Mann (7)

Graham James Primary School, Corringham

Magic Land

Magic Land is in the sky,
It's in the clouds way up high,
You can see sparkling unicorns,
They even have bright pink horns.
In Magic Land rainbows shine day and night,
The sun also shines bright,
Giant crystal walls surround Magic Land,
The friendly fairies will even give you a hand.
The magic is very strong,
We are always having a sing-song.

Paige Louise Willis (7)
Graham James Primary School, Corringham

Football Boys

S port Land is very funny
P ut a ball in the sports goal
O h, Sport Land is very fun
R ats on their way to Sport Land
T ea for a person to drink

L ittle boys watching football
A nd a whole bunch of boys walking to it
N ever sad times it's always happy
D addy went to football smiling.

Billy Webb (7)
Graham James Primary School, Corringham

Football Land

F razer loves football.

O h, football is fun!

O h no, I missed a game!

T ottenham are good.

B alls are hard.

A mazing football.

L ots of fun.

L ots of football.

L ovely football.

A goal keeper.

N ail a goal.

D on't lose a game.

Frazer Wilson-Green (7)

Graham James Primary School, Corringham

Ninja Land

N injas train all day
I n the forest and after training they play
N o one can skip training
J amie would make it start raining
A ll day people smile

L ater on they end up in a pile
A nd they said hooray
N o one likes the day
D o you like my land, it is in my hand?

Anthony Rawles (8)
Graham James Primary School, Corringham

Sweety City

S weets are nice,
W ow, I want them in my tummy,
E verything is nice,
E veryone likes sweets,
T reats are tasty and good,
Y ummy treats are great,

C hocolate is so yummy,
I cing on cakes is great,
T reats are so lovely,
Y ou will love these treats.

Lucas Gibson (8)
Graham James Primary School, Corringham

Boy Land

B oy Land is very smelly,

O n the dirty river water there are fishermen fishing,

Y ou can enjoy burgers, hot dogs and chips.

L ate at night we stay up and eat treats,

A nd in the cities there are big buildings,

N o girls allowed!

D angerous cliffs surround Boy Land so be careful!

Jake Hurst (7)

Graham James Primary School, Corringham

Chocolate Land

C hocolate is so amazing

H opefully people like glazing

O pening chocolate is so great

C oming to Chocolate Land at the best rate

O reos are so yummy

L ater on they're in your tummy

A fter you are full

T he waterfall is so cool

E nd of the day, time to play.

Ronnie Jay Garland (8)

Graham James Primary School, Corringham

Football Land

F ootball Land is nice and dirty,

O pen the land and off we go,

O pening football presents so we can be happy,

T ackling rough and playing in the mud,

B alls are everywhere,

A ll people are watching to have fun,

L ots of stadiums,

L ots of people buying footballs.

Samuel Munro (7)

Graham James Primary School, Corringham

Dino City

D ino City is good fun.

I ndominus Rex is a killing machine.

N ot many dinosaurs like people.

O f course they love to eat.

C ity of dinosaurs is very cool.

I n my world you can look at dinosaurs everywhere.

T -rexes are strong.

Y es Dino City is the best!

Jamie Vice (8)
Graham James Primary School, Corringham

Candy Land

Candy Land is very yummy,
I wish I lived here with my mummy,
The houses are made of lemonade sticks,
Usually made from big brown bricks,
It rains Skittles, Smarties and M&Ms too,
There is a gummy bear kangaroo in the zoo.
The monkeys say boo and make me jump,
It is half past twelve and I have the hump.

Ruby Fitzgerald (7)
Graham James Primary School, Corringham

Dino Land

D amp caves everywhere

I ce nowhere to be found

N o pretty city

O ld dinosaurs

L izards dying everywhere

A llosaurus in a fight, allosaurus won't win the fight

N ights are tough

D ilophosaurus, very small dilophosaurus, very cruel.

Max Bridges (8)

Graham James Primary School, Corringham

KFC Land

K FC is the best,
F ried chicken tickles your chest,
C ooper, my cousin, loves chicken breast,

L ands around the world are good,
A nd mine is better to visit, I mean you should,
N anny and Grandad, everyone eating,
D on't forget the KFC song.

Teddy Vallis (8)
Graham James Primary School, Corringham

Burger City

I hear burger birds sing,
I see people shouting.
I see some people talk,
As I walk.
As I arrive to Burger Park,
I had a mark
Of burger sauce on my top.
As my balloon popped,
As I saw a burger tree
And I touched a burger bee.
Come and see my city,
It is very pretty.

Joshua Cannings (7)
Graham James Primary School, Corringham

Bubble City

I hear bubbles popping
And people are hopping,
I see luxurious buildings,
All around me in the cities
I smell smoke flavoured bubbles
And people are having huddles,
I taste niceness in the air,
Because it's *magical!*
I can touch a building brick
When I kick.

Tyler Griffiths (7)
Graham James Primary School, Corringham

Dinosaurs Are Great

D inosaurs are great

I ndominus rex is weak

N ot many dinosaurs like people

O f course they love to eat

W ow this world is sure great

O wen is a dinosaur keeper

R oar!

L ands are awesome

D inosaurs are big.

Henley Jackson (7)

Graham James Primary School, Corringham

Boy Land

B oys and fun
O n their special island
Y oung boys go on adventures

L ook at the beautiful sea
A nimals are scary and live in the woods
N ever feed the fish in the sea
D ance around the campfire on the big and huge mountains.

Lukas James Shawyer (8)

Graham James Primary School, Corringham

Ice City

I n my city it is fun,

C hildren playing until the day is done.

E veryday it snows.

C hilly mornings,

I lay in bed all wrapped up,

T ime to wake up and have a snowball fight,

Y ou might get a fright.

Lexi Ridgewell (8)

Graham James Primary School, Corringham

Jurassic Minecraft World

All of my world is made of blocks
and also there are rocks.
There are dinosaurs everywhere
and some have lots of hair.
It is all sunny.
The dinosaurs are acting very funny.
So come to my city.
Because it is very pretty.

Charlie Finch (8)
Graham James Primary School, Corringham

Underwater City

As you swim,
You can follow him.
Beware of the shark,
Especially in the dark.
There are lots of fish
On the dish.
It is a city,
That is very pretty.
The submarine is very fun,
Especially when the day is done.

Daisy Adela Anderson (8)
Graham James Primary School, Corringham

Unicorn City

Every unicorn is nice here,
I taste yummy gummies,
I see ten unicorns dancing,
I hear a neigh from far away,
I touch two on my way,
I can smell tasty treats to eat,
I love Unicorn City,
It is very pretty.

Georgia Unwin (7)
Graham James Primary School, Corringham

Roblox World

Roblox World, ever so crazy,
Over there is a lazy daisy,
They all looked very good,
But now they are all in a hood,
I think 'Coolgameboy' is the best,
But definitely not that guest!

Marco Eric Minter (8)
Graham James Primary School, Corringham

City Craft

C heerful, happy place,
I n the middle of an island.
T imid rats, elephants and unicorns.
Y ou will see it's magnificent.

C olourful by day, black by night,
R eally amazing, you don't have to pay,
A big giant will come and pay.
F or you it has really good KFC, it's the best.
T hey have really amazing buses to take you
there.

Joshua Maxwell (10)
Hedgewood School, Hayes

Minecraft

M inecraft, the blocky fun game,

I n Minecraft, building houses is awesome,

N ow in Minecraft we have new cool mobs,

E nemies look dangerous,

C rafting objects may be catastrophic,

R avines will be enormous and dark,

A lso white chickens are able to fly,

F ireworks can be mixed with deadly TNT,

T rees have weird brown bird's nests.

Marcel Wyrzykowski (10)

Hedgewood School, Hayes

My Imagination

M y world has Zomburbia, suburbia and moon bases,

Y ou will be amazed.

W ith Oggy's house and Freddy's pizzeria

O utstanding Zombopolis and trials of gnomes

R avenous is how you'll be in Freddy Fazbear's pizzeria

L icensed to build this place is what I am.

D ecisions were made to build this unusual place.

Zak Bhad (11)

Hedgewood School, Hayes

PJ Ninja Paradise

In PJ Ninja Paradise,
Fearsome PJ masks fight crime.
In PJ Ninja Paradise,
The masters of Spinjutsu save Ninjago.
In PJ Ninja Paradise,
The sarcastic PJ masks get captured.

PJ Ninja Paradise smells like cotton candy.
PJ Ninja Paradise glaring in the starry night sky.
In PJ Nninja Paradise,
I can touch the houses from the beautiful night.

Chris Byrne (10)
Hedgewood School, Hayes

Miraculous Ladybug In France

Miraculous Ladybug in France,
Can see you in a glance.
PAW Patrol and Mickey will be here in a jiffy.
Powerful and fantastic music, very mystic.
Shimmer and Shine to help me rhyme.
Gleeful and cheerful, everything is beautiful.
Doc McStuffins goes to bed with muffins,
While they sleep you won't hear a peep.

Emma Sofia Walsh (11)

Hedgewood School, Hayes

Sweet Land

In my land everything is joyful,
My eyes can see a gleaming land,
My nose can smell delicious fruity sweets.
My tongue can taste red candy, yummy!
My ears can hear happy kids,
My hands can feel the chocolate melting,
Everything is funny!

Mohamed Jama (11)
Hedgewood School, Hayes

The Golden Temple

I see the Golden Temple of Amirtsar.
I can hear the beautiful Indian music.
Touching the spotless ancient floor in the temple.
I can smell the wonderful spices of Indian food.
I can't wait to taste the healthy yet pleasant food.

Rocky Verma (11)
Hedgewood School, Hayes

Chinacraft

In China everything is so busy,
There are big, high awesome temples,
There are tall, impressive mountains,
Cliffs and boulders that are stuck.

Sam Fletcher (10)
Hedgewood School, Hayes

The Land Of The Little

There was once a man,
Who was very poor,
In fact he slept in a sock drawer.
It was a world of magic, colours and smells,
And with him he kept a little gold bell.
It was his good luck charm,
Along with his lip balm.

There was an old lady,
With two pet hares,
And the three of them lived under the stairs.
It was dark and dusty and awfully loud,
But the little old lady was still very proud,
She grew mushrooms in a large pot,
And she and the hares ate the lot.

Then one day the two of them met,
He was going for a stroll,
And she was going to the vet,
He said, "Hello," and she said, "How do you do?"
They chatted and laughed and then time flew.

They talked of stairs, hares, charms and lip balm
And their love did no one any harm.

Soon they married and found their forever home,
They no longer wanted to be alone.
They moved into a mouse hole,
It was warm, pleasant and very cosy,
And now their lives are merry and rosy.
With pictures on the walls and love in the air,
They truly are the happiest pair.

Ophelia Ruby Tucker (9)
Ingatestone & Fryerning CE (VA) Junior School, Ingatestone

Harry Potter And The Horcruxes!

Welcome here to Hogwarts castle,
Where the wizards perform spells and owls deliver parcels.
Here you learn to make wonderful potions,
Some will give you good or bad emotions.
Harry says the seven Horcruxes need to be found,
In order to defeat Voldemort without a sound.
The first Horcrux is Tom Riddle's diary,
But be careful in the chamber as it could be fiery.
The next one is Marvolo Gaunt's ring,
Let's find this bit of bling.
The third Horcrux is Salazar Slytherin's locket,
When Harry finds it he will put it in his pocket.
Helga Hufflepuff's cup is the next one to find,
But be careful of Bellatrix, she is not kind.
The fifth Horcrux is Rowena Ravenclaw's posh crown,
Which would have looked lovely with her gown.

It's a shock, Harry Potter is a Horcrux as well,
Quick, go to Hogwarts and ring the bell.
The very last Horcux is Nagini the snake,
He needs to be caught before he slithers back to
the lake.
Harry has them all and Lord Voldemort is now
gone,
He is happy and so are his friends Hermione and
Ron.

Ruby Ann Kendell (9)

Ingatestone & Fryerning CE (VA) Junior School, Ingatestone

Rainbow Day

In Rainbow Land, everyone loves Rainbow Land,
It is bright, colourful and grand,
All the colours have a job to do,
Including red, yellow and even blue!
Red is the police and enforces the law,
And tells you off if you don't do your chores.
Yellow is the heater and keeps it warm,
Especially when it's raining or a heavy storm.
Pink tidies up and makes everything clean,
It's the prettiest land you've ever seen.
Blue keeps everything healthy and keeps himself wealthy,
Orange is a teacher and likes to learn new things,
Their favourite project is to dance and sing.
Purple is the cook and loves to bake,
Who doesn't love the rainbow milkshake!
Green is the gardener, an important job indeed,
But don't be afraid if you're a weed.

Tegan Barber (7)
Ingatestone & Fryerning CE (VA) Junior School, Ingatestone

Treasures Of Spring

I was enveloped by the sparkling treasures of
spring,
As I stepped back to observe I felt like a king,
A carpet of bluebells were dancing in the breeze,
Though I couldn't help but admire the lovely
emerald trees.

The verdant grass was tickling my toes
And the smell of barbecue wafted up my nose.
The harmonious song from the birds could be
heard miles away,
As the sun sets on the horizon, I have to say
goodbye to my day.

Flowers: red, yellow and blue,
Plants blossoming that are all brand new.
Trees wearing their suits of bright green,
New flowers sprouting that have never been seen.

Sophie Thomas-Scrine (11)
Ingatestone & Fryerning CE (VA) Junior School, Ingatestone

Sisters

Sisters are sisters, we never get on
And we're always moaning if one of us is singing a song,
We fight over things that don't really matter,
Like arguing and shouting instead of a chatter,
Sisters are sisters, we like to have fun,
But instead of saying nice things we call each other dumb,
Sisters are sisters, no matter how tall,
Sisters are sisters, even if they're small,
Sisters are sisters, we have the same mother,
Sisters are sisters, we also have a brother,
Sisters are sisters, if they don't seem to care,
But if something happens they will always be there.

Ella Farrow (11) & Ava Farrow (9)
Ingatestone & Fryerning CE (VA) Junior School, Ingatestone

Candyland

I woke up one morning and I saw
A huge florescent tree with a bright purple door,
When I walked through the door to my disbelief,
The mountains were cakes
and what's that? A candy cane thief.
The thief ran across the mountain cakes
And he swam across the icing lakes,
Until a woman came out shouting, "Thief!"
I chased the thief through the woods
And I raced the thief as far as I could.
Then I brought the thief to a station
And the police man asked for an explanation,
While I walked home as happy as can be
But this is a secret only for you and me.

Orla (10) & Darcie Earp (10)
Ingatestone & Fryerning CE (VA) Junior School, Ingatestone

Football Dreams

I think and dream of football
I think of it at school
To me the game of football
Is brilliant and cool

I like to think of playing
In front of all my friends
And being the star player
In a game that never ends

I imagine I'm the goalie
I put in some good saves
And all around the pitch
The fans shout out my name

I play football in the sunshine
I play it in the rain
But I'm just a schoolboy
And I'll dream and dream again.

Jenson George Wiles (8)
Ingatestone & Fryerning CE (VA) Junior School, Ingatestone

Underwater Oceans

Underneath the sand,
Is an undiscovered land,
With many other creatures of the world.
Down in the blue,
Lives a goldfish or two,
Trying to find their way around.
It's a beautiful place,
With a rough sandy base,
There's seaweed that grows on the floor.
While mermaids glide,
The fish hide
And the predators own even more.
Now here's a description,
That's probably fiction,
That starts from the edge of the shore.

Emily Sutton (10)
Ingatestone & Fryerning CE (VA) Junior School, Ingatestone

Candy Galore

In this world of Candy Galore,
Are sweets of plenty and more and more.
There's a cocoa river
And gummy worms that slither.
There's not one single brick in sight,
Though caramel can hold tight.
The sweeties that fall from the trees,
Will make you fall to your knees.
The big gummy bears that live in the wood,
Could eat you up whole, really they could.
I hope you've read this, well and good,
And embraced this candy hood!

Poppy Edwards (10)
Ingatestone & Fryerning CE (VA) Junior School, Ingatestone

Friendship Land

Without a friend I'd be down,
Without a friend I'd have a frown,
We have fun in the friendship sun.

In the friendship sky, way up high,
We follow the friendship rule
And dive in the friendship pool.

We follow a straight path to a warm friendship
bath,
Together we go to see the heartbreaking view
And see a spider collect its friendship dew.

This is my wonderful life in Friendship Land!

Imogen George (7)
Ingatestone & Fryerning CE (VA) Junior School, Ingatestone

Butterfly

Look at the butterfly,
What do you see?
Gentle and delicate,
Just like me.

Starts as a caterpillar,
Makes a cocoon,
Suddenly a butterfly,
Flying to the moon.

They come in all different colours, shapes and types,
But most of all just like moths they like lights.
This butterfly is as pretty as a rose.

Saffron Alexandra Burrows (7)
Ingatestone & Fryerning CE (VA) Junior School, Ingatestone

Flower Fun!

F lowers are amazing!

L avender absorbs your eyes.

O rchids are a sweet surprise.

W ater lilies are like stars.

E nglish bluebells are nice in a vase.

R oses curl up and hide from the sun.

S nowdrops and all are for everyone.

Ariana Knight (7)

Ingatestone & Fryerning CE (VA) Junior School, Ingatestone

The Land Of My Imagination

In a land where the gummy bears glow,
And where the chocolate rivers flow,
Where skeleton pirates swim,
Underwater in the dark and dim,

Where dinosaurs shoot black snowballs,
Where you see how the flying squirrel falls,
Where the candyfloss trees stand,
Although the floss tastes salty but bland,

There is also a king who rules this land,
His castle is made up of sugary sand,
The land of my imagination is a fantasy world,
Where untold secrets are wrapped up and curled.

Ziyan Khan (9)
Longfield Primary School, Harrow

Candy Land

C ome see my dream come true, next time it could be you.

A llow the magic of my land to fill you with joy and laughter.

N o questions asked, nothing to fear, just mischievous monkeys to look after.

D on't miss the flying gummies, but most important is the candy bomb.

Y ou can indulge in a milkshake pool, so many flavours to choose from. Beware that if you come to stay, you may not want to go away.

Umika K Bhula (8)
Longfield Primary School, Harrow

Candy Land

My land is full of candies and sweets,
A land to behold,
So colourful; to eyes a treat.
The trees in my land are lollies,
Packed with apples, oranges and zingy heat.
The houses have walls made of chocolate bars,
And roof made of caramel sheets.
The roads are covered in liquorice,
That seems to melt under Haribo sun's heat.
So if you come to my land
All you would want to do is eat, eat, eat!

Isa Khan (8)
Longfield Primary School, Harrow

The Land Of Lollipops

Lollipops, candy canes, fill my world with joy,
Oh, every adult wishes they were a girl or a boy,
Lots of people come round to stay here,
Lucky people are here since there is no fear,
In my planet everything is free,
Popping candy to KitKat Chunky,
On my planet there are seven moons,
Perhaps you may see me in my house of balloons.

Ayden Alam (8)
Longfield Primary School, Harrow

Future Land

In Future Land,
Everything's grand,
People have enough food,
which keeps them in a good mood,
Driving cars,
Can take you to Mars,
Robots give us a helping hand,
So we can play in the sand,
Our planet is alive and well,
What more is there to tell?
Here I am in Future Land,
Would you like to lend a hand?

Shiven Patel (8)
Longfield Primary School, Harrow

Space Candy Land

In Candy Land,
It is so sweet,
You don't need to ask to get a treat,
Candy Land is super neat.

Once the man goes to space,
He unpacks his grey old case,
The man starts to dance with grace,
What a lovely place, space!

Mili Jackson (10)
Longfield Primary School, Harrow

Cow

C lever
O utstanding
W onderful.

Eamon Aichaine (10)

Manor Mead School, Shepperton

Cow

C lever

O dd

W obbly.

Arun Dodson (11)

Manor Mead School, Shepperton

Smiggle City

S un shining in the sparkling daylight

M agic happens in Smiggle City, blue birds tweeting happily

I stand on the wavy grass as I watch the sun go down

G randad planting flowers as colourful as the rainbow

G ardens filled with joy as bubbles float through the air

L emurs dancing in the circus as everyone cheers on

E verybody's happy in this city.

C ats bouncing around with joy

I see squishy water bottles being squirted at people

T ime goes slow in Smiggle City

Y ou have to come to Smiggle City where everything is pretty!

Olive Yardley (8)

Rolph CE Primary School, Thorpe Le Soken

Horse World

H orses can be seen galloping round the fields.
O ver jumps they bound, elegantly flying.
R osettes lined up calling for the winner.
S addles and stirrups of silver and gold.
E questrian sports fun and exciting for all!

W onderful horse cases with treats for the good.
O nwards they charge, serving in the battle.
R iding on horse back round the city.
L ong, flowing tails blow in the wind.
D iamond encrusted reins made for a princess.

Jessica Arnold (8)
Rolph CE Primary School, Thorpe Le Soken

Rubik's Land

R ubik's Land,
U p high the humongous Rubik's Cube buildings tower,
B ring along some Rubik's power and fun,
I can see a big humongous, hot Rubik's sun,
K ids playing on them everywhere,
S ee I can solve 3 (4 x 4, 3 x 3, 2 x 2),

L ovely land,
A mazing Rubik's pathways,
N ever are they failing,
D o you like them?

Toby Hamer (7)
Rolph CE Primary School, Thorpe Le Soken

Love Magic Land

M olly is cuddling her Mum and Dad.
A magical unicorn is helping a friend.
G arden creatures happily playing.
I ndian people dancing.
C andy is yum in my tum.
A mber is friends with India.
L ove is nice.

L ove is kind.
O pen my heart to love.
V alentine's love.
E lves making presents for people.

Amelia Jane (8)
Rolph CE Primary School, Thorpe Le Soken

Time For Nightmares In Nightmare Land

Coffins the size of houses,
Monsters are big and scary,
Be careful, they are behind you!

Ghosts, silent as a mouse,
Vampire's teeth are pointy and long,
Be careful, they might bite you!

The blood as red as apples,
Spiders as big as your head,
Be careful, they might jump at you!

This is what nightmares are made of,
Ha, ha, ha, *boo!*

Avier Jackson (8)
Rolph CE Primary School, Thorpe Le Soken

Candy Land

Candy, candy, candy,
Lovely, sweet candy.
Skittles, fudge and candy canes,
Lovely to eat on a candy train.

Candy clouds and raining sweets,
Candy cows and multi-coloured wheat.
Gingerbread sweet as nectar,
You can eat it in all weathers.

Candy schools
And caramel sticking walls.
Candy cane trees
And fitting candy cane keys.

Oscar Hudgell (8)
Rolph CE Primary School, Thorpe Le Soken

Chocolate Land

Chocolate buildings can be seen towering across
the kingdom.
I can smell the aroma of freshly cooked chocolate
cake, straight from the oven.
The mellow sound of the chocolate river as it
passes through the kingdom.
Chocolate scent, so powerful.
I can taste it as I walk the chocolate encrusted
streets.
As the smooth, brown rain begins to fall, I stick my
tongue out.

Orson Sibley (7)

Rolph CE Primary School, Thorpe Le Soken

Cake Kingdom

I can see buildings made of different coloured cake, some tall like a wedding cake.
Walking through the pathways you can taste cake scents flowing into your mouth.
Crunching, crackling can be heard and I can hear people baking cakes.
The smell when walking through villages flows up into my nose.
I can feel cake homes and pathways.
I love my world!

Hannah Francis (8)
Rolph CE Primary School, Thorpe Le Soken

Architect Land

I can hear hard workers knocking down towering, beautiful homes.
The smooth taste of the strawberry, apple and mango rainbow cake as it touches your lips.
The smell of mango, apple and strawberry rainbows being made into juices. Mmm!
Designs can be seen from towering hotels.
I touch the silky outline of my home.
It just can't get any better!

Rosey Hawkins (8)
Rolph CE Primary School, Thorpe Le Soken

Animal Kingdom

I hear dogs barking in the beautiful, peaceful
meadow.
Everywhere I turn I see animals that are joyful
around me.
A mile away cats can smell a warm, fishy ocean
flowing into their mouths.
In a house of animals I taste a warm, lush scent
flowing into my mouth.
I touch every animal's fur around me.
I love Animal Kingdom!

Isla Weston (7)
Rolph CE Primary School, Thorpe Le Soken

Toy World!

T oys are for free
O h, come before they run out
Y ou can't wait for toys

W hat a dream to have so many toys
O h this is a dream come true
R eally, what a treat for toys
L ego and L.O.L. Dolls looking for a home
D inosaur rubber stand on a book.

Ava-Rose Clark (7)

Rolph CE Primary School, Thorpe Le Soken

Lifeboat Land

L ifeboats go splashing out to sea,

I n lifeboats brave people stand,

F lying out to sea to rescue lost people,

E ager to save lives,

B oats sinking are rescued,

O ut they launch into the water,

A good team,

T raining to become a proper lifeboat crew.

Isabella Thachter (8)

Rolph CE Primary School, Thorpe Le Soken

Race World

R ace World is my world
A race goes on every day
C ars racing and horses racing
E verybody racing

W orld's biggest race
O f course the horses and cars are fast
R ace when you want to
L eaves look like race cars
D o you race?

Zac Hewitt (8)
Rolph CE Primary School, Thorpe Le Soken

Freddie Rusbridge (8)

Rolph CE Primary School, Thorpe Le Soken

177

Dragon Landia

I smell the scent of smoke, for smoke dragons they aren't far.
I feel the wetness of water dragon's spray.
I taste the dragon sticks when they feed me every day.
I hear the cracking of eggs when the cloud dragons hatch.
I finally see everything which is...
Dragon Landia!

Seb Woodcock (8)
Rolph CE Primary School, Thorpe Le Soken

Chocolicious

Melting mountain,
Beautiful bite,
You can fill my tummy with all your delight.

Chewy and gooey,
Perfect in cake,
After that you make my tummy ache.

Perfect with custard and cream,
Cream and custard are nice,
But chocolate, you are my life.

Millie Rawlinson (8)
Rolph CE Primary School, Thorpe Le Soken

Rainbow Dust

I smell sweet, green trees growing.
I always see wishing fairies visiting children.
I love to touch a huge unicorn cake straight from the oven.
I taste yummy fruit sweeties falling from the sky.
I hear horse riders clipping saddles on unicorns.
I love rainbows!

Emilia Jayne Hall (7)
Rolph CE Primary School, Thorpe Le Soken

Unicorn Land

I hear unicorns trotting along the grass.
I see unicorns flying high in the sky.
I smell perfume coming from the unicorns.
I can taste the fruity rainbows.
I can touch magic of the unicorn horn.
Unicorn Land, a magical land to be in.

Savannah Brinck-Davis (7)
Rolph CE Primary School, Thorpe Le Soken

The Magical Land

(A kennings poem)

Colourful mountain
Magic sparkler
Sparkle spinner
Hand glimmer
Pretty maker
Grass sparkler
Magic glimmer
Castle glimmer
Pop slimmer
Sparkly river flowing
Amazing trimmer.

Nicole Susan Moore (8)
Rolph CE Primary School, Thorpe Le Soken

Art Land

In Art Land everything is pretty,
You can make glittery glitter paint,
You can make your own art,
Your work will be shining with glitter
And you can smell the bright scent of flowers.
I love art!

Sienna Morgan (8)
Rolph CE Primary School, Thorpe Le Soken

Zombie

G oing into horror
A nd scariness
M y favourite thing is Resident Evil Biohazard
E ndings of zombie games
S oon blood will be spilt.

Danny Tooneear Kelly (7)
Rush Green Primary School, Romford

Mario

M usic box and
A pples in Mario Land
R ock stars playing music
I want to sing a song
O range tricks.

Tiago Roddrigues (8)
Rush Green Primary School, Romford

World Of Magic Wonders

Unicorns can fly,
Mermaids can swim,
In this magical world,
Action men can sing,
Abracadabra alakazam!
Make this magical world for me.

Instead of clouds it's candyfloss,
Instead of school come on over,
To a party of ecstatic laughter,
All your time will disappear faster,
Tick-tock, tick-tock!

Reg Barrett (10) & Devon Moran

Sacred Heart Catholic Primary School, Ruislip

Yay, This Is A Random Place To Be!

If the queen had a choice to see this land,
she would say, "Oh dear, oh my, I'd rather sink in quicksand."
For you see our visitors come in a very large variety,
as we have an extremely strange society.
If we had a party,
it would surely be super arty,
and if you were to look up into the sky,
you would see syrupy pancakes flying high!
So just listen to the boombox,
can you hear it sing Tegan and Sara's singy thing?
There are lost mugs running about,
asking, "Anyone seen a map hanging around?"
There's Len Goodman saying, "Seven," up to the heavens.
See this land is so random,
most don't know whether they're standing
on the floor or on the sky,
But this world is so random it surely does not need a sign!

Hollie Jessica Banister (11)

Saxon Primary School, Shepperton

The Land Of Time

When was Mr Time born and when will his powers
end?
I live in a world where every second is a minute,
every minute is an hour, every hour is a day, every
day is the same.
The mistakes going over and over again,
Like a broken clock, like Big Ben,
When, oh when will it end,
I'm down in the centre where things never get
better,
But I like it that way,
If it's all I can choose from.
Make a mistake and you will never forget,
Like Mrs Dumbee,
She lost her cat and I lost my hat,
We will never have these things again.
As I said I just go to bed knowing what I wake up
to in the morning,
Now enough of that, look I can even see you
snoring,
Because I know my world is boring.

Isabelle Willoughby (10)
Saxon Primary School, Shepperton

Dreams In The Sky...

The land of sky,
It is all mine,
Here fairies fly,
No one shall cry,
For creatures here,
From far and near,
Do good,
As much as they possibly could.
The Sugar Plum Fairy rules the land,
Where sugar lies instead of sand,
Where rainbows stretch from cloud to cloud:
They're bridges! Don't you understand?
I know this world sounds strange, untrue,
"Oh well," is all I'll say to you,
Imagining is my profession,
And here to you, is my confession,
Oh yes, this world is my creation,
Oh yes, it's my imagination.

Vika Nekhaenko (10)

Saxon Primary School, Shepperton

Winter's Miracle Island

It is that time of year again,
When the crackles of the fire keep you warm
And the sparkles of snow entertain,
Winter's near...

The robins sing their morning chorus that the poor
can enjoy,
Meanwhile the rich have their tea party,
Singing, dancing and having fun,
Not even noticing the unfortunate.

Sleeping in their boats with no protection to be
found,
The dismayed cannot bear the cold,
It is winter all around!
Carols are sung by children and parents of one.
On the island of the winter's miracle
It is winter every day.

Lucy Taylor (11)
Saxon Primary School, Shepperton

Your Sweet Dream!

Wonderful candy lay flat on the ground,
In a world that is still somewhere around.
If you look to your left then right,
This will appear to be an amazing sight.
Then you can fly across the gummy sea
And maybe see a gummy me!
So come along and join the fun,
In Candyland that is number one.
Snack on candy like you have never done before
Because it's a place I know you will adore!

Chloe Palmer (11)

Saxon Primary School, Shepperton

Winter Wonderland

Everyone is happy with the snow falling down,
Snowballs and snowmen are all around.
The elves are making presents
and mums are buying carrots for the snowmen,
Santa's wrapping presents ready for Christmas
day.
The milk and cookies are on the fireplace ready for
Santa.
At the end of the day,
People are in blankets,
Ready for Christmas Day.

Alfie Sumer (11)
Saxon Primary School, Shepperton

Pirate Island

For most sail the seven seas...
There are some who do not agree,
As the souls a victim of raid,
They will never be repaid
But the beautiful, sunny, islands hide the dark truths,
Their beliefs intoxicate the once innocent youths.

Besides all that,
Grab your sails and drift away
in the glorious oceans of Pirate Island...

Logan Phillips (11)
Saxon Primary School, Shepperton

Woodland

Plodding through the dank mist,
In a place with no paths,
Shadowy trees, hauntingly still,
The damp air whispering of decay.
I pause and listen. Silence,
Only a single drip from a lone willow.
I look on
And there ahead was a stream of willow tears.
Is that a bridge?
No, just a fallen trunk, all rotten with fungus.
I pause and listen.
A shriek from a crow,
I glanced in the direction of the *caw*.
A streak of water stretched motionless,
I draw closer.
No, not water,
A path of pebbles.
I quicken my pace,
Curious for what's to come.
A glimmer of orange and a hint of smoke.

A homely amber light spreading through the dull murk.
A cottage!

Amélie Shearer (11)
St Cedd's CE (VA) Primary School, Bradwell On Sea

Flamingo Land, Love Land

F lamingoes flourish beautifully here
L ove is a plenty, peace everywhere
A ll the time the shimmering sun is shining
M ists of pink covering the land
I ntelligence and beauty is everywhere
N o harm, no unkindness
G rowing freely, palm trees sway
O n the salty calm lake, flamingoes stand

L ove is amazing and speaks its own language
O rigami love hearts made every day
V isually it's a place of true love
E verlasting, flourishing and peaceful.

Love flamingoes!

Kelsey E Loerns (11)
St Cedd's CE (VA) Primary School, Bradwell On Sea

Candy Land

The chocolate rivers are flowing,
The sweet grass is overgrowing,
The flaming red lollies reaching high in the sky
Are a real spectacle to the eye.
As the children pick the sour laces from the ground,
The young chocolate birds are singing a sound.

The toffee and caramel house is rather icky
And the windows made from boiled sweets are very sticky.
So why not come and see the chocolate river and dip your feet
Because Candy Land is a real big treat!

Chloe Guy (10)
St Cedd's CE (VA) Primary School, Bradwell On Sea

Marine Life

M ost of the time when you think sea you think fish,

A nd I admit they end up upon your dish,

R ound, flat and thin,

I n China they eat canned shark fin,

N ow let's set sail for the sea,

E mperor angelfish are calling me.

L uminescent sand glowing in the rolling tide,

I t's going to be a bumpy ride,

F ind a seahorse, I shall do,

E lephant seals dive into the ocean blue.

Rhianna Richardson (10)
St Cedd's CE (VA) Primary School, Bradwell On Sea

Fun Football

F un and excitement around the football field.

O ver-exaggerating about all of the tackles and free kicks.

O n the pitch, goals, penalties and other offsides.

T all and small people competing in the match.

B rilliant skills makes a brilliant player.

A mazing passes and delightful dribbling.

L ovely sunshine glistening through the sky.

L ucky goals and shots soaring through the sky.

Thomas George (11)
St Cedd's CE (VA) Primary School, Bradwell On Sea

Gummy Town

In Gummy Town,
It will not make you frown,
Everything is filled with laughter,
There's even a chocolate master crafter,
All of the treats are full of joy,
And there even is a jelly bean boy,
There's a chocolate river,
Where all the gummy worms slither,
So come and visit the palace,
Where you can stuff your face,
Then I suddenly return from my dream,
And then shoot out a smile that will beam.

Poppy Newby (10)
St Cedd's CE (VA) Primary School, Bradwell On Sea

Winter Park

Twelve, midday, to the skatepark,
Down the road, through the gate.
Me on my BMX, look to the right,
See my mate, check my text.
Look ahead, see the concrete level bed,
Half-pipe, spine and rails,
No room for errors, trips or fails.
The air is cool, the park is dry,
Boards, bikes and scooters echo all around
Time to make some air and leave the ground.

Cian Thomas (10)
St Cedd's CE (VA) Primary School, Bradwell On Sea

Dream A Big Dream

As I close my eyes to sleep,
I see the story of my life appear in my mind,
I feel my future in my head
And the happiness in my heart,

I hear my voice saying to me...
"Your life is getting better,"
But the most important thing it's saying to me
Is "Thank your parents as they give you your
dreams!"

Sian Eley (10)
St Cedd's CE (VA) Primary School, Bradwell On Sea

Underwater City

My underwater city,
The floor is wet and gritty,
Everyone travels in submarines,
Which are speedier than runner beans,

The houses and shops are made of metal
And all around the seaweed settles,
To go for a walk you wear a space water suit
And all the dogs wear small silver boots.

Theo Brown (10)
St Cedd's CE (VA) Primary School, Bradwell On Sea

I Am The Ocean

I am the ocean
I do not boast
About the great power
That I hold.

I do not care
About what lives in me
Because should an ocean really care?

Never ask me any questions
Because I am the ocean
Is it really worth it for me to listen?

Emma Tamar Lamb (11)
St Cedd's CE (VA) Primary School, Bradwell On Sea

The Mysterious Forest

Deep in the forest where nobody went,
I wanted to explore why the branches were bent,
Thoughts filled my head of what it could be,
I scurried along so I could see,
There in the distance it was as plain as can be
And that will forever be the mystery.

Jessie Lipscombe (10)
St Cedd's CE (VA) Primary School, Bradwell On Sea

My Land

M y Land is full of friends.
Y ou can be in my land.

L and of magic.
A nd pirates to be found.
N ever getting bored with all the celebrations.
D reams come true.

Dennis Cooch (10)

St Cedd's CE (VA) Primary School, Bradwell On Sea

Piggy Park

On your 13th birthday
You get a nice surprise,
A pigalicious piggy
Hidden right inside
Of a beautiful blossom,
On the apple-meg tree,
Adopt a piggy today
And help set it free.

Cars? Cars?
What are they?
We use piggies every day.

Now here's the sad part of my world,
When someone here turns very old,
Ninety-nine to be exact,
They start to feel freezing cold,
The pig they own and care for
Starts to stiffen and turn to stone,
For an ornament for their grave
Or something in their warm, stone cave
To treasure forever and ever.

Harriet Olivia Dann (10)
St Peters CE Primary School, South Weald

Dream Dessert

In a world of dreams
Everything is quite unique
From many colours galore
To candy scattered on the floor
Houses made of birthday cake
And sugar sprinkled over lakes
It rains bows
It grows glitter
It has unicorns picking up litter
Puppies can fly high in the sky
Kitties can talk and sing on high
Candyfloss clouds
And happy miaows
Every time you blink
Your house turns a different shade of pink
So come and join all the fun
For there's always space for someone not to be
glum.

Poppy Holder (9)

St Peters CE Primary School, South Weald

The Land Of Good Fortune

In the Land of Good Fortune,
State your desire,
But wish something evil,
And be consumed by fire,

Will it be flowers or bees?
Or an orchard full of apple trees?

Give me some puppies,
And a sea full of gummies,
Mmm, that's yummy.

So now you know,
All about the Land of Good Fortune.

Eshan Jarvis (10)
St Peters CE Primary School, South Weald

My World Of Words

In my world of words,
There is everything, even birds,
Everything that pops into your head,
Is going to have to be read.

Everything is made of words,
Even those sweet Nerds,
Words make the ceiling,
Words make everything but feelings.

No bad words aloud.

Isabel Slaney (10)
St Peters CE Primary School, South Weald

Marshmallow Land

Welcome to my land, come and eat sweet treats,
Where everything is marshmallow, there's a
chocolate river.
This is a magical world, come and eat sweets,
This is not a dream, come and eat the best sugary
sweet you will ever meet.

So what do you say, stay or come?
Well, if you come you can find all the gems
And the mellow marshmallow princesses
Will make you the marshmallow queen.
Have a sundae with a shake,
A marshmallow shake with caramel on top.
When it rains, it's marshmallow rain with cream on
top.
Your bed's so soft, in fact it's a scented
marshmallow ball with cream.
You won't get sticky, it's just scented.
So give it a try?
Or stay in your boring, unexciting land.

Brielle Minta (8)
St Teresa Catholic Primary School, Dagenham

Zombie Apocalypse Land

Z ombies, oh the smell of rotting flesh, disgusting, ew!

O n the highway witches everywhere.

M aniacs trying to rip my brains out!

B e faithful and I can defeat these beasts.

I really need some weapons to help me!

E w, the disgusting smell of week-old brains.

A dd my power and get stronger and stronger.

P eople will think it's a horror movie but it's reality!

O h no, no a nightmare skull has spotted me. Aargh!

C ome on I've got eighty-five lives.

A h, if only I could slay the mother, I would be the *king!*

L ie down, pfft! Never! I need to gather resources.

Y es, all of them: titanium, uranium, diamonds and iron.

P lease, the mother stands no chance.

S lay, *cut, boom, clap, clap, clap!* The mother is slain.

E asy-peasy lemon squeezy, king here!

Lucas Cretu
St Teresa Catholic Primary School, Dagenham

Fashion Town

In Fashion Town everything was found.
Everything was pretty, just like the city.
They buy fashionable things every day
Because they are comfortable every day.
If you wear the clothes,
You are not allowed to tear the clothes.
Hurry up you are going to be late!
You don't want to miss the cake.
Let's go to the park!
Let's get into the car.
This is all ruined
Because of you, we can't even do it.
Why is your jaw open,
All because the door can't even open.
Watch out for your daughter
She is getting closer and closer,
You just hit your head on the car,
Well that was funny,
That must have been hard.

Cherish Chiziterem O'kasi (7)
St Teresa Catholic Primary School, Dagenham

Imagination Land

In Imagination Land everything is pretty.
I sleep in a cosy Skittle bed
And the sky is still gummy like a gummy bear,
Everything is good, not one thing is bad.
You can eat whatever you see because it's made out of sweeties,
So that's why everyone has a tummy ache when they get home.
When I sleep I'm not warm, I'm colder than ever
I'm posh but not that posh,
I wish but not every time,
I'm wise but not too wise so that's why I'm happy every day,
When it's dinner I say, "Candy, candy, where's my candy!"
After that I go to bed in my cosy bed.

Toni Osoba (8)
St Teresa Catholic Primary School, Dagenham

Looking Land

L istening to everyone and looking at nice things,

O h, night and day I travelled far away,

O h look! A knight coming towards me!

K icking through the night and looking like a knight,

I look at everything like a royal knight,

N ight through day I travelled in Looking Land,

G rowl at bad things and be nice to good people,

L iking nice and good things,

A nd Looking Land is the best!

N ow let's look at Looking Land,

D ads are fun and mums are fun so let's go to Looking Land.

Benas Taujanskas (8)

St Teresa Catholic Primary School, Dagenham

Cherry Blossom Land

Cherry blossom, cherry blossom,
Where are you?
How do you do?
Be, be, be,
You are my best friend,
How ferocious you smell,
I will remember my roots,
I'm a little girl, I like smelling flowers.

I love flowers,
Flowers will make me laugh,
I will refresh my body and spirit,
I love flowers, they remember me,
They love me and my spirit,

Flowers are precious like roses,
They smell lovely too!
They make medicine for people who are sick.

Toluwa Lateef (7)
St Teresa Catholic Primary School, Dagenham

Magic Land

Magical creatures, oh so beautiful
Waterfalls sparkle in the sunlight
Furniture made out of candy
And the mermaids have a banquet at night

Magical wands sparkle brightly
Unicorns are around
Diamonds are shiny
Magical carpets even go underground

Portals are always purple
Fairies in the air
Rainbows you can walk on
Peaceful and so many lairs
You live in diamond castles
It rains jewellery, money and gold
So many accessories to choose from.

Christine Kirumbi (8)
St Teresa Catholic Primary School, Dagenham

Maths Land

I love maths it is the only thing I never let go,
Sun shining bright in the sky,
Maths, maths is everywhere!
The moon is maths in the sky,
Only if you know bikes and the love inside you.

People ride in rectangles trains into stations,
Money, money only in trees
If you take them they will never grow again!

Beautiful shapes for you to take!
They are lovely shapes! Go and buy them!
Wow it is amazing! Remember go to the land today!

Marcela Gnaczynska

St Teresa Catholic Primary School, Dagenham

Rich Land

My land is very rich,
It's like a football pitch,
It has more than one million dollars
and more than one trillion dollars,
I like cash
But I'll get money in a dash.

I like posh clothes,
But I love quotes.
We buy sports cars
And we can buy some darts.
I love Rich Land
But there's still beans in a can.
My land is rich
But I get money quick.

I like rich games
Because I really want fame.

Courtney Chiagozikam O'kasi (7)
St Teresa Catholic Primary School, Dagenham

Rocky Man Rainfall Ender Land

Bonjour, welcome to my land,
Which is crazy and wonderful and raining Oreos,
You can eat a nutshell which has nothing inside it.

The trees and rocks look awful,
There's a house with lots of giant food,
But you are little.

There is a nutcracker and a goblin,
You have to attack them before you get the
diamond mine cart.

The aeroplane has a cheeky face,
It never comes off,
When people see the face they run away.

Teddy Benton (8)
St Teresa Catholic Primary School, Dagenham

Whirl And Twirl Land

You will be dizzier than a tornado,
The twirl dragon is as fun as a kid,
But the twin bunnies are as cute as a baby,
It is as hot as the sun.

There's no school like Tobago,
You will float like balloons,
The candy is as sweet as love,
There's a clown funnier than puppets,
The beach is as fun as a party,
It never rains like Kenya,
There are diamonds like stars,
And crystals like glitter.

Sophie Attard (7)
St Teresa Catholic Primary School, Dagenham

My Land

Shimmering glitter falling down like snow from the sky.
Sunny days shine in the sky, that makes me smile.

The joyful crowd in the town,
It makes me shout hooray.

Chocolates are yummy, they fill my tummy,
I can dance when I'm happy.

Singing is what I do best,
It makes my mum have a rest.

I'm worst at tap in my class.
I'm trying my best to get it right.

Marlena Gnaczynska (8)

St Teresa Catholic Primary School, Dagenham

Rain Land

In Rain Land it rains like it is flooding.
The trees are so big the sun can't come out.
The plants are nice and healthy,
The animals drink lots of water.
It is like a huge maze,
People cannot cut down the trees.
Lakes and rivers are very popular,
The water's like a flood.
Everyone loves Rain Land!
The people use umbrellas.
Maybe one day you would like to come to Rain
Land.

Matthew Akinseye (8)
St Teresa Catholic Primary School, Dagenham

YOUNG WRITERS INFORMATION

We hope you have enjoyed reading this book – and that you will continue to in the coming years.

If you're a young writer who enjoys reading and creative writing, or the parent of an enthusiastic poet or story writer, do visit our website **www.youngwriters.co.uk**. Here you will find free competitions, workshops and games, as well as recommended reads, a poetry glossary and our blog.

If you would like to order further copies of this book, or any of our other titles, then please give us a call or visit **www.youngwriters.co.uk**.

Young Writers
Remus House
Coltsfoot Drive
Peterborough
PE2 9BF
(01733) 890066
info@youngwriters.co.uk